Indirect Light

T0282115

Also by Malachi Black

Storm Toward Morning

Indirect Light

Malachi Black

Four Way Books
Tribeca

i.m.
Paul Matthew Campbell

&

to F.

Copyright 2024 Malachi Black
No part of this book may be used or reproduced in any manner without written
permission except in the case of brief quotations embodied in critical articles and
reviews.

Library of Congress Cataloging-in-Publication Data

Names: Black, Malachi, author.
Title: Indirect light / Malachi Black.
Other titles: Indirect light (Compilation)
Description: New York : Four Way Books, 2024.
Identifiers: LCCN 2024000681 (print) | LCCN 2024000682 (ebook) | ISBN
9781961897120 (trade paperback) | ISBN 9781961897137 (epub)
Subjects: LCGFT: Poetry.
Classification: LCC PS3602.L32 I53 2024 (print) | LCC PS3602.L32 (ebook)
| DDC 811/.6--dc23/eng/20240111
LC record available at https://lccn.loc.gov/2024000681
LC ebook record available at https://lccn.loc.gov/2024000682

This book is manufactured in the United States of America and printed on
acid-free paper.

Four Way Books is a not-for-profit literary press. We are grateful for the assistance we
receive from individual donors, public arts agencies, and private foundations including
the NEA, and the New York State Council on the Arts, a state agency.

We are a proud member of the Community of Literary Magazines and Presses.

Contents

IV.

It is easy to descend into Avernus.
Death's dark door stands open day and night.
But to retrace your steps and get back to upper air,
That is the task, that is the undertaking.

Virgil, *Aeneid* VI

Two forces rule the universe: light and gravity.

Simone Weil

I.

For the Suburban Dead

How can I mourn them? My books should
lift up from their shelves and become doves.
Or should I tear down the walls themselves

to grave-pit level? Having passed through
the convoluted plumbing of the long
pneumatic tube that swallows all

beginnings into one glass after-
noon, I turn the lock to my apartment
no less stung, no less befuddled

than a tourist exiting the subway
uptown when the map had let him
run a sure, confirming finger

to the south. There are palm trees
in the city where I now cross
against the lights, dodging traffic

from another kind of life: rented
bikes, electric scooters, touring
diesel-powered trolleys shuttling sun-

burnt souls back from the waters
upon waters of the broad Pacific coast.
Always aboveground, always going

east of freeways, west of mountains,
I shield my eyes from the white sky
and slide cold beads across the mind's dark

abacus: eleven years, five states,
as many break-ups, six apartments,
and one season in a vacant summer

home. In the layering of days between
my curtains and their last New York
borough window, I have learned to hold

the loneliness of cities in my teeth
like old fillings. I cross the street
and cast the shadow of a matador

lifting his cape against the wind's
untethered ghost. Each year, another
far-flung friend falls in a hole

cut like a tunnel to the overcrowded
underworld, only to be covered up
by clods of soil. I would lay myself

down like a flower on each headstone
if I could, but I have lost the plot
numbers, and, anyway, my face

has so much changed that I would
startle like a ghoul. How could it be
otherwise? In the imperceptible

arrival of each instant as it passes
through the permeable membrane
of the last, I am so busy being

grafted to the greenness, for example,
of just-mown grass, that I forget
the folding over of my skin—

collapsing in slow motion, bending
out while creasing in—thus seeming
always to myself both old and young.

I'm neither one. I cast my glance
some sleepless early mornings
to the east. In those vast hours

of evaporating dark, I can become
a stillness in the spaces between
stars. But then a cold light burns

another night from the horizon.
I watch it die. There, in the smoky
cobalt distance, I can almost see

the staggered stock chart silhouette
of old midtown Manhattan, where
the Empire State Building spikes

the skyline like an insulin syringe.
The clouds above its hypodermic
spire flicker red. I turn my head.

Look: from the curb of every corner
on the island, and all precincts
crosshatched out beyond the river

borders of its grid, the needle
is as much a landmark as it is
a promise or a pledge: the last

vaccine for mortal loneliness.
Doctor, your bag is being carried
through the doorways you just left.

I was a patient once. Now I have traded
pallor for a tan. And yet my friends
lie blue-lipped in cold basements,

scratching at the other side of rest
with startled eyes and children's hands.
Father, Mother, you know that

I have nothing to confess. How
then can I hope to be forgiven?
Scabs. Burnt spoons. Gnawed leather

belts. Hospital tubes. Hospital
gowns. Hospital beds. Doctor,
turn back. One of us lives.

Indirect Light

i.m. Scott David Campbell (1982-2012)

Streetlights were our stars,
dangling from the midnight
>> in a planetary arc
above each empty ShopRite
parking lot—spreading
>> steam-bright
through the neon dark—
buzzing like ghost locusts,
>> trembling in the chrome
trance of an electrical charge
nested in each exoskeleton—
>> pulling, pooling
a single syllable of light
from the long braid
>> of the powerlines
sighing above us as we climbed
through bedroom windows
>> with our hair combed
and our high-tops carefully untied—
as we clung to vinyl siding,
>> crawling
crablike across rooftops, edging
toe-first toward the gutters
>> so as not to rouse

the dogs—as we crept down
onto cold drainpipes
                        through the lightning
in our lungs, leaping at last
into our shadows and at last
                        onto the lawn,
landing as if in genuflection
to the afterhours fog—
                        fluorescent
as the breath we left
beside us on the train tracks
                        as we walked
each toward the others
and the barebulb
                        glow of stardust
on the dumpsters
in the vacant late-night, lost—

Old Polaroids (Pictures from a Graduation)

So this must be the color
of the past: a light as amber
as the whiskey in my glass,

the ice long melted. There:
a tint of antique paper
in the unsuspecting air

embellishes the silhouettes,
yellowing the glare
into a jaundice.

Like dinner silver tarnished
to a patina of brass,
each shine has lost its polish

in the drawer where it was left:
the teeth, the tightened eyes, the hair,
the flash caught in old eyeglasses

once noted for their stylishness,
now clownish, graceless, brash.
Some things are ugly simply

for their earnestness. We stand
in for ourselves, arranged
like storefront mannequins

left in their window years after
the business has collapsed:
our faces blanched, our gazes

dead behind the glass. We look
but can't look back. From time
to time, an aging passerby

looks in. He frames his fading
face with jaundiced hands. His
eyes are blank. He squints.

Into the Mouths of Saints

Lord, I am
stung: your name
        crisp as a wasp
upon my tongue,
        I blister, lame

less than I am
        numb from
wanting. Clenched
        as the mantis is,
I knelt in dust,

        stuttered open,
full of throat
        and pulse, each
red cell swollen
        like the locust's

husk with longing:
        but *O*, hollow
vowel, hum
        of the bare folds
of the breathless

lung, your prayer
has emptied me
        of breath begun
in calling: all
        I know above

me is the echo
        of my own
voice, baffling
        the absence
of reply.

La Vita Nuova

We sang along. Our first night
almost gone, we broke the rusted

hull of your Corolla through the snow-
fall with one dead headlight and iced

wiper blades. Sixteen and too old
for home, we held the shoulder

on Route 80 West, riding
the spasms of the rumble strip

to Sparta, Netcong, Newton, Hope—
hand-rolling bags of Bali Shag

as empty FM stations foamed
a static thick and bright and steady

as the snow. You drove, guiding
the steering wheel with one thigh

while I stroked a marijuana finger
from the frayed sleeve of my camo

coat, and when the gaslight signaled
on the dashboard, your palm sweated

in my own. We know these snowdrifts
shifting into dusk, shadows sprung

like tusks out of the pines half-
buried overnight by snowplows

weary of the interstate. We park,
letting the engine run, our tailpipe

flicking its exhaust in tongues
across the unwatched asphalt

of St. Peter's lot. Our hands
are laced together, and they glow

like new magicians' gloves, fluttering
above the slow heat of our bodies

in the backseat dome light as we
churn, and slur, and hum. The radio

is low, but something like a chord
takes hold, and my salt trembles

into yours. Another dense flake
melts onto the hood. Too soon,

your womb will coil with a vine
fed of our blood: a clotted son.

May he curdle there and wither
like the curse still on my tongue.

Help me, Rhonda: these are words
you know by heart. We are young.

Your mother was in high school
when she named you for a song.

Mother-of-Pearl

Or so I'd name you, lost scrap
of the sky, ghost of wrinkling
water on the checkered kitchen

tile, swirl of wet grasping light
inside each bubble clustered
on the cold lip of a milk glass,

iridescent white but magnified
and magnifying, bright as an ice
skating rink in the afterhours

dark, present but transparent
as the shadow of a swimmer
cast across lake-bottom rocks,

shy as the glimmer of a new dime
dropped in the patched grass
in the park, quiet as an eyelid

as it shuts, nightwise, after love,
as yours, stranger, does,
while I whisper to myself

another name, a little gauze
to wrap the pale trace you will leave
inside the morning, like a fog.

Indirect Light

i.m. James Scott Latona (1982-2017)

No taller than a mother's
waist, we bubbled shoeless
                    through damp August
haze, squealing sweat-
soaked and grass-stained
                    into the vacillating
spray of rusted lawn sprinklers—
suspended in the echoes
                    of our names
above the stiffly crewcut
sod, our small backs arcing
                    upward and away
from each faded brick facade
in our unmanicured
                    apartment complex—
our bright sounds skipping
off the surface of the yard,
                    clapping in ricochet
against the mold-flecked
shutters and cracked paint
                    of single-parent
window frames—our vision
rippling with the asphalt
                    distance, blurred

like the watery inscriptions
of nearby dogwood branches
                    dipped in shade—
our street-scabbed bodies
briefly tinseled in the sun,
                    fathered by the light
we gathered and the light
we gave back to each other
                    one by one,
all of us lunging forward,
sliding faster through the mud—

Greystone Park Psychiatric Hospital, Late Spring

Like voices in the rain, our names
have curled into themselves
a clinging mist. This

is as memory insists:
a sense of what must be
lifts from the edge

of what has been, and rests
inside the present
as a hinge. My brother

flinches, gone, or gone again
into a schizophrenic rift,
rocking like a blade

of grass swept by the strange
April wind, no more tethered
to the past than to the bed

on which he sits. I won't
visit him again. I've hurried
all I can remember

through a long fluorescent hall
to wait inside the air
cleft by his name. He runs

his palm against the lantern
of his head: a shadow
falls, a shiver frightens

off the wall, and he dissolves
into a perfect tense
between the shadow present

on the wall that I perceive
and the static past
the wall that he reflects.

Lines from the Throne of Old Ideas

Self: What is the substance of a mind?

Soul: Fireflies in a pickle jar.

Self: Is time a circle or a line?

Soul: Moth wings tapping on a drum.

Self: Am I the water or the fire?

Soul: Steam uprising from the soil.

Self: What, then, of the afterlife?

Soul: A coil of air, a curl.

Entering Saint Patrick's Cathedral

I have carried in my coat, black wet
with rain. I stand. I clear my throat.

My coat drips. The carved door closes
on its slow brass hinge. City noises—

car horns, bicycle bells, the respiration
of truck engines, the whimpering

steel in midtown taxi brakes—bend
in through the doorjamb with the wind

then drop away. The door shuts plumb: it seals
the world out like a coffin lid. A chill,

dampened and dense with the spent breath
of old Hail Marys, lifts from the smoothed

stone of the nave. I am here to pay
my own respects, but I will wait:

my eyes must grow accustomed
to church light, watery and dim.

I step in. Dark forms hunch forward
in the pews. Whispering, their heads

are bowed, their mouths pressed
to the hollows of clasped hands.

High overhead, a gathering of shades
glows in stained glass: the resurrected

mingle with the dead and martyred
in panes of blue, green, yellow, red.

Beneath them lies the golden holy
altar, holding its silence like a bell,

and there, brightly skeletal beside it,
the organ pipes: cold, chrome, quiet

but alive with a vibration
tolling out from the incarnate

source of holy sound. I turn, shivering
back into my coat. The vaulted ceiling

bends above me like an ear. It waits:
I hold my tongue. My body is my prayer.

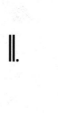

II.

Holding a Book I Haven't Read for Many Years

I lived once in a burned-out Ford sedan.
I knew only the make; its ornament
stood, bald and undaunted, on the hood,
but its word, the block script of its model,
had been pried off by the junkyard hands
of a drunk vandal, or perhaps just lost
to dirty weather and the rising hunger
of a purifying flame. I knew this
as I myself had first been made and then
remade by the raw force of the elements,
my name spoken and sung until it was
a claim broken and spun like the clear web
of a spider hanging from the rearview
mirror of a burned-out Ford sedan.
The doors were crippled in or soldered shut,
but I could bend and lever my thin bones
over the windowless side panels.
I slept in the back seat like a bad thought.
Or tried, turned on my side and counting
each bright shard lodged within the galaxy
of cracks in the front windshield. I was young;
all signs were still, to me, illegible.
I strained my eyes, blurring to mist each form

drawn by the dark, scanning the horizon
for a movement, some trace of living code,
a mark, and then found none: only the vague
cone of the moonlight as it broke like chalk
against a blackboard. I was alone;
the nights were slow. And so I gave myself
back to the duct-taped bench seat, summoning
breath out of bent spring and crumbling foam.
I wanted a new sacrament. Still proud,
I was a child king in a paper crown
ceding his power to a parliament
of clouds. Their shadows marbled the windshield
as I looked through my reflection looking out:
the eye inside the eye reading itself
inside my private hall of mirrors
on the chassis of a burned-out Ford sedan.
I rode the circuit of self-reference.
Then I fell back, exposed, a runaway,
teeth chipped, unclean, lips cracked, lifting my gaze
as if tilting a telescope, and saw,
indelibly, at last, beyond the wind-
shield and its whorl of shattered glass, beyond
myself, beyond the veil, beyond the blank

moon spinning in its trance, the infinite
extension, intergalactic, edgeless,
incomprehensible as distance,
dimensionless, as indivisible
as measureless, unraveling itself
out of itself enclosing, opening,
enfolding knowing and unknowing,
expanding like an unrestricted lung—
and so it was. I shuddered breathless,
risen up, quickened but suspended
in a vertigo above the junkyard
planet wheeling in its carousel
of rust under a burned-out Ford sedan.
Released from equilibrium, I saw
the world unwind the substance of its forms
from the half-light, each shadow being
absorbed by the young sun. And then I felt
the meaning of it fall from me, a shiver
of lost knowledge blown off by the wind
of some new life: each intimation
skidding on Earth's surface like a page
torn from the cracked binding of the book
I hold tonight in my rough hands. With age,

the ink has been effaced; the words are changed
to apparitions, dim impressions. I trace
each withered symbol where it fades, but what
I see, I can no longer understand.

Indirect Light

i.m. Laura Elizabeth Allocco (1979-1999)

Blue as a swimming pool,
the cold ghost of the morning
                        held a coin
of early light, and we clenched it
in the lashes of our bulbed,
                        half-open eyes—
our faces creased and swollen
from the sleep we'd left
                        inside, still
gathered in the polyester
folds of blankets splayed
                        on bunkbeds
we despised—our bowl cuts
damp from bathroom faucets
                        where we paused
to rake our cowlicks before
stumbling outside—our brows
                        flattened against
thickset station wagon
windows, trapping the fog
                        from each pale breath
expanding only to contract
its cataract across the carpool's
                        blurry filmstrip—

frame by frame, the daylight
flickering its shadow-puppet gods
                    onto the almost
mirrored walls of our tempered
parallelograms of glass—always
                        the distance closing
far too fast, the liquid motion
slowing, our bookbags' mouths
                      pouting open
on our laps, our hangnails
reaching to the handle, opening
                      the latch, the school
day's alloy tongue hammering
its bell to call us back—

In Our Late Empire, Pride

drops from upper air,
                    like rain,
clinging brightly
                    to the fresh-cut hair
of children
            and the infantry:
all hail
        the clicking heel, all will
regale
        the shrinking light
with grains
            of wedding rice, or salt,
or sand as fits
            a last brassy parade:
the marching band
                    will soften
with its growing-distant
                    drum,
the oscillating hand
                    must stop
its waving
            soon enough, soon
enough;
        for now, the motorcade

hums

      gaily through the citizens'
applause

        and the children's eyes
bronze faintly

          with the glint
of far-off fireworks,

            or firebombs,
or sinking evening stars.

Narcissus at the City Pool

The arm that reached up from the water
seemed his own, but it was colder

and it shivered to the touch: wrinkling
at the surface as if meeting with his

fingertip alone had made it old,
rippling the skin loose from its bone

in woozily reduplicated folds
like cigar smoke, almost a ghost.

He paused. Was it the underside
he saw there, risen up? Or was it

something more: a future born
of half-translucence, given form

to draw him down, steady the hand
that he drew back, and pull him in?

Indirect Light

i.m. Jillian Lee Loreto (1983-2001)

Bloodshot through the fallen dusk,
our eyes glittered like fish scales
              in the shallows
of the wet back-alley scum—
our spray-paint nicknames
              glistening
in gold above the wilting
silhouettes of cardboard boxes
              and torn trash
bags scattered by the rats
we startled, crouched over
              their inkblot
holes—our bodies bent
down in a denim hush, low
              voices folded back
and forth across the dry buds
of our molting tongues—
              teasing weeknight
stars out of the leaky twilight
with damp matchbooks
              as we learned
to swallow sparks—sucking
flame through homespun spliffs
              and limp unfiltered

Pall Mall cigarettes we'd counted
out from staling soft packs
                    left in parents'
bedside drawers—slackening
our backtalk jaws to coax
                    each cumulus
of smoke up through our nostrils
and then down as onto spools
                    held in our lungs—
our muffled laughter scissoring
the purple dark, climbing
                    beside us
up the thin rungs of a fire
escape and rippling skyward
                    as we lay
our giddiness against the still-
warm rooftop tar—our far
                    eyes shrinking
the distance to the space junk
satellites, impossibly alive
                    and blinking
their dusty dead bulb
sockets back at us—

A Dispatch from the Last Stout Elm in Chatham's Fair Mount Cemetery (N.J.)

Here, too, a tablespoon of light
spills from each temporary star—

to filigree the green blade
of a leaf's edge in the dark

tree we have climbed
as if to merge our bodies

with the names carved
in the bark: Archie, Janey,

Daphne, Clark, the hearts
you closed around a sapling

have since slackened, gray
and oblong, like elastic

in an old man's sock—
ageless, almost, as we are,

squirreling higher up
to where the branches fork

the air untouched
by the unbearably pure

glare of a police squad car,
our sweatpants pockets full

of pills and stolen pearls.

Bloodlines

Night circles like a dog above its bed.
I whisper to the moon, a bent spoon

bubbling like a tiny saucepan
in my still unsteady hand. Stretch

out, bold claw, relent: each scab
embedded in the skin inside this elbow

is a freckle kept from childhood,
as on the ceiling I have kept

each swollen glow-in-the-dark star.
Tonight I borrow from Orion

one pin prick and a buckle for the belt
I tighten like a choke-chain on the ghost

in my left arm. Pisces, Aries, Canis, Crux—
where can I find the pale astronomer

who'll trace these constellations
from the ripple of my blood?

Morristown Memorial

i.m. Paul Matthew Campbell (1952-2021)

Your neck is Staten Island–tan, your hands
are strong, your biceps taut, and you can almost
sing, Beezy, as you bend into the midday
rain. It's July. Watergate is front-page
on the *Times*: America, again, is in
decline, and it's just 1973.
But what's a crime? You lift the collar
of your fringe leather jacket against the wind.
In stride past the newsstand, each step ripples
calf-high through the draping of your bright blue
denim bell bottoms, and the wet street beneath
your boots shines like the moon. There is no hope
like yours, billfold flush with construction job
cash for the flat-topped cop who downcycles
dope to the street corner freaks who'll spend
another summer on the nod. He winks;
you pay. Past the ferry lies Manhattan,
that Island of Fast Toys, ruby candy
lights, and the Lower East Side studio
where Gail, your new girl, lines incense cones
along her windowsill. Even in the rain,
your boot heels seem to spark all the way
to Tompkins Square up from the Battery.
There is no part of you that knows, nor can

believe the cruelty of the bloated, half-
blind body you will heave, gowned and your own,
onto a gurney at the Morristown
Medical Center on New Year's Eve
2013, and in the absence
of that knowledge bends the shadow
of the god to whom I pray. Gail waits,
blowing a piece of lint from an old LP
she lays upon the turntable, its needle
opening an unreal panel in the wall
to the Dave Brubeck Quartet breaking down
"Take Five" on the last reel at Columbia
Records when your mother was still a goof
bored in a chrome booth at Mel's malt shop
and Nixon was Duckpin's VP. But times
have changed, and love hangs like a disco ball
over the warped linoleum of the hall
down which Gail's mumu sways. You knock, entering
her room of song, carrying an air of calm
and slipping off your boots in two smooth motions.
Gail leans back on her cot. You wrap your rain-
slick leather fringe around a wire hanger's
sagging shoulders, then bend your lips to hers.
You grin. You run your tongue along this prelude

and its promise: that you shall make the world
a church. Unclasping the thin brass buckle
of your braided belt, you kneel before Gail's
TV table. Bowed in practiced reverence
to ritual, you light a match and lift
it to the wick of a lone votive candle.
Slowly, deliberately, with an altar
boy's cautious solemnity, you unfold
Flat Top's stamp-sized glassine envelope.
You tap the bag, teasing half its powder
into a burnt-black soup spoon, then dip
the tip of Gail's syringe into what water
waits still in the glass she keeps at night
beside the cot. You mix, coaxing the spooned
serum to a steam, stir once, stopper up,
and tie Gail off. Only when her head bends
softly to the side do you presume
to administer the blessing to yourself.
And as the rising summer of it swells
through you like cicada song, you lean
back into a phantom gondola
to ride the astral rowing of your blood.
Beezy, you sleep. Inside the undulations
of warm dream, Brubeck is your gondolier,

your guide. You idle down the East River,
slide past the Bay. You see the city shrink.
Then you rise, effortlessly, like a wind-
swimmer over the monstrous Mobius
strip of Jersey roadways, rinsed pigeon-gray
by the rain of July 1, 1998.
You tour, and glide, and course the overhead
until you swim down to a curb. There,
as through a basement window, thirty-three
miles due west of Gail's OD, who is it
that you see, skeletal and trembling
beside you in a metal folding chair
at an NA meeting on the water-
stained flooring of the Calvary? It's me.
You hand me coffee in a paper cup
with powdered cream. Your belly bulges
through a button-down. Your eyes are summer
blue and beckoning behind a pair
of wire-rimmed frames. Your freshly barbered
hair is gray. Your neck is tan, your hands
are strong, your biceps lean. You wisecrack
and heave back, Beezy, bellowing a laugh
in cool fluorescence. Your fake teeth gleam.

Lines Written on the Slats above This Steel-Framed Bottom Bunk [First Day in Detox]

If it is
emptiness

that lifts
a buoy

above
the sotted

waterline
then let me be

as empty
as the sky

III.

A Letter from the End of Days (Come In. Clean the House. We Have Died.)

Unscrew the door, but leave the knocker.
Wrench the latch from the brass key.
Pluck the doorstep from the bushes;
pull the bushes from the weeds.

Clear the curtains. Draw the cobwebs.
Wring the water from the tea.
Clap the stairwell from the carpets,
tease the plaid out of the sheets.

Brush the books, now, from the dustshelves:
Let the brittle pages flake,
and in the snowfall of confetti
on the floorboards, write your name.

If you have come and there is winter,
trim the glimmer from the snow.
If you are here and it is summer,
sweep the sunset from the stone.

Take the birds down from their branches;
none of them can sing. On the fire
line of the horizon, fold and hang
the wilted ashes that have gathered

like white flowers in the black fields
of their wings. Trace the dry veins
in the soil, where the runoff once
cut cold; in the dimples where the rain

fell, plant the smallest shards of bone.
As the night wind comes unraveled
and the cracked-skull moon begins to swing,
lay your head against the gravel

with your hands over your face.
Earth will buckle in its seizure,
cleaving crag to gorge; rock spray
will surge up from new fissures

in the desert valley floors.
Rasping sands will lift and coil
from the separating dunes
and wrap into a thickened funnel

sucking surface from the flatlands
like smoke into a flue. Now call out
to the mountains, beg for respite
from the stars: there is nothing else

to help you. There is no one here
at all. Even this letter you have,
written in your own ensorcelled
hand, flickers coldly and dissolves.

Dulce et Decorum Est

Fuck the construct of my reverie.
Fuck the wilted head of cabbage

I mistake for a symbol of the egg-
yolk yellow sun. Fuck the stilted

blue jay and the branch its feather
breaks: slow white pulp foaming

like old milk out of a straw. Fuck
cells still grafted to the enervated

blank of a God that's always now
or long since gone. Fuck the rust

that bubbles through the cold shell
of black paint along the spear points

on the cemetery gates, and fuck
the constant suction of raw time:

each second clustered in the steam
from my lost breath, each minute

rising through my body like the last
smoke from the coals of a bone fire.

In Our Perishing Republic

Their watches tick. Their eyes are as they were
when they went slack: as sallow as carved wax.
The dead lie frozen in their mothers' cars.

Their fathers cough, rising from cloth armchairs
to shut off a kitchen light. The faucet drips.
Their watches tick. Their eyes are as they were,

watching *Late Night*. A buzzing streetlight flickers
at the curb: a strobe over black ice.
The dead lie frozen in their mothers' cars.

One neighbor calls for a loose dog, another
looks through the blinds. A hall clock chimes.
Their watches tick. Their eyes are as they were

after a last glass of grenache. Their doors
are locked. Wind swings a flashing traffic light.
The dead lie frozen in their mothers' cars.

They bear syringes in their outspread arms.
They lean back. They are parked in the wrong lots.
Their watches tick. Their eyes are as they are:
the dead lie frozen in their mothers' cars.

Horoscope (Presentiments of the Abyss in Mitchell, South Dakota)

Translate the tin squeal of the weathervane
back to rust. It's not the wind's dark carousel
that spins the dented arrow toward a voice
you know you heard, but something in the claim
itself—an animal complaint—that rises
through the feathers of the crows above the barn
to churn the leaves and stir the dust and turn
the world. Its vowel shivers in your wrist.

Begin again. Lay day on top of day
like face cards from a half-unshuffled deck:
the king of clubs, the queen of spades, the jack
of hearts, his coldly pharaonic eye
forever bending from the beveled axe
blade at his neck. Mark this: indignity
is blunted by indifference. To meet
the bright blank of the future, turn your back.

Lines from the Ninety-First Floor

A fantasia

I have been given
        what I never asked
to see: the airborne
        pigeon vivisected

by the scissor
        of an airplane's
wing, the bird's
        eye open, wholly

open to the half-
        beat of its severed
vein, suspended
        midway, only

momentarily
        between the purling
updraft and
        a sudden slack

unspooling
        in the flightpath's
string: as if
        the bird were being held

before it fell,
      as if the act of being
halved itself
      had set the bird against

its fall no less
      than flight: as if the bird,
in being briefly
      still, found second life.

Through the Pastel-Powdered Light (Cape Cod)

Word came like a quick rain—
whispers, a soft knock
              on the warped, mossy wood
some long-ago forager
planed for a front door—
              and we emptied the dark
apartments of our selves,
thinking nothing of scarves,
              thinking of nothing
but cigarettes and socks,
boots and old binoculars.
              Past the crooked inland pines,
through tufts of dune grass
and driftwood pale as birch bark
              under early morning cloud-shadow,
we hurried up a sandhill—
five unsteady sets of eyes—
              and finally stood still, breathing
hard toward Herring Cove
and a pod of twenty, thirty,
              maybe forty blue-gray bodies
close enough to swim to
from the shore. They splashed—
              like penguins in a bathtub—

slapping, thrashing, roiling the sea
into whitewater, breaching, each

                arcing all of its ninety tons
above the horizon, then lifting
glassy flukes to gull-level

                in the sea-sprayed air.
We said nothing. We saw
whale, water, air, and each other

                as if through a glass eye.

To Cicero's Hand

They cut you off, let fall your hammered silver
bracelets to the sand. Then, wrapped in cloth
rougher than gunny sack, you were cinched

tightly with a dexterous twist of braided,
double-knotted hemp. Swung back against
the saddle's end, knocking eighty miles

on the lathered haunches of a swaybacked mare,
you bled into the little sickle shadows
in old hoofprints up the Via Appia.

In Rome, they hailed: and fixed you, wrist-
wise, with a nine-inch nail, to a gray beam
of the Rostra in the public square. So it is

written. Why should I care? Today, the air
is warm, the park is rippling with children,
and squirrels flirt on lush, protected grass.

An ice cream truck's tin song gathers its notes
back from the wind. I shut my eyes. Time is
a static in the mind. And I'm caught in it

still, trying to forget the ravaged dead.
Opening my eyes, I see you, withered hand,
and finally I know the arc of history

is webbed: the lines in my palm are crossed
with yours now—half-folded, crooked, cramped—
held out as if in warning. *We are hexed.*

Coda: Sehnsucht

What am I now? Another vow to keep

fresh lilacs in the house, or just the sound

of one who learns, after so long, to live

without them? All that I've had, I've left

propped up in a glass vase: cut stems

at rest within a thin preservative

of sugar water tipped with vinegar.

They look so still. They ask for nothing

but an interval, opening only

for the rough span of the vowel lost

from *root* to *rot*. I watch them wilt: they were

borne here to be killed. But what of the hands

that stirred, almost above themselves, like wind-

swung birds, to coax the buds into first flame?

New Year's Letter to Li Bai

How long is the wind?
It strings the blue bead
of the earth in place
from end to end.

Say it is one piece
in a necklace, then
what jeweler? What neck?
Star-eater, you said

nothing when I asked;
you couldn't hear me
with my mouth pressed
to the galaxy's

black ear. Or did you
turn to read my lips,
watching the dimple
of each syllable

form then disappear?
The wind spools each word
back onto its string,
opening another

silence on the lip
of the horizon
between mind and thing.

Pharaoh's Last Glance at the Nile

Yes, it is a terrifying thing to have been
born. But in the impress of the elements

along the delta mud, where water wrinkles
like loose fabric in the sleeve on a boy's arm,

the sun-quenched earth, pierced and partitioned
into seedbeds by the spade and the moon's thirst—

what other suction draws the bloated monsoon
clouds for summer floods?—glows like the golden

eye of Horus, god and hawk. Such is our crop,
so thick the linseed in alluvium as soft

as oiled calfskin, it may be that our worms
are angels tapered for the soil. Even the birds

have bread; they fatten daily on the loaves
from baskets heavy on our heads, and still we have

coarse barley for the goats, grains stacked on the grains
left for our slaves. This is the ancient sanction

of the silt and river sand: the silos overflow
into our hands. Our bodies have been molded

in the image of our gods to coax the wheat
and split the fig and sift the corn. Who doubts

the power of a nation where foods ripen on demand?
Our temples all are risen, as our streets, out of the land,

and we must yield to what we have—as the butcher kneels
to tend the throat of each warm lamb. The constellations' wheel

sharpens itself above our heads. Reaper, whet the sickle's edge:
the harvest of our kingdom is a season without end.

Indirect Light

i.m. Kathleen Roche (1982-2018)

God of all comfort, close
your hand over the tract
                    houses of Livingston—
lay shadow on the subdivided
land of Christmas lights
                    and cul-de-sacs
and minivans—withdraw
the mortar from the bricks
                    that bind the staggered
townhomes and cracked
chimneys over white-trimmed
                    condominiums—
swallow the mailboxes
down into the loam beneath
                    each quarter-acre
lawn—pull back the plots
of mulch and patchwork
                    sod until they spill
like sewage through the streets
and brim the tunnels under
                    Morristown, South
Orange, and East Hanover—
strengthen the cold, crooked
                    bones that mold

the undertaker's glove
as his fingers smooth the satin
                    lining of the pillows
in the caskets where the dead
lie faded as old rugs—soften
                    the rocks lodged
in the subsoil for the digger's
dented spade—brighten
                    the headlights
on the hearses as they bend
down turnpike exits, leading
                    another mute
procession to the cemetery's
rusted fleurs-de-lis—ice
                    the puckered
calla lily petals in green
sympathy bouquets, raised
                    so they glint
like winter trumpets
in the echo of no sound—
                    as freezing rain
rests on the headstones
and snow falls underground—

IV.

Prayer of the Last Prizefighter

                  Small god of the sea
glass, imp of riverbanks and everyweather,

give back to the sand this knuckle-shrapnel
and the hand that rattles like a snake's tail

with its loose shards of bone. Let the star
whose dead light leans against me be my last

enemy: may my opposition be
as phantom as the shaft of its cold beam,

collapsible as ash is to the touch.
Surrender me to shallows and the salt

gallop of a rising surf, to the dark
burrow of the mole crab and the snail shell's

supple purple curve; scatter to the gulls
these teeth chipped by the lifting surge

of uppercut, eyes lost in their own whites,
this tongue still swollen with the pulp

of its old blood. Little lost god, hidden
dizzy in the driftwood, I leave to you

this lip split by the language of half-luck:
though I was formed of two parts water, one

part dust, I was born before the first
light of the sun. I know death

is man's divinity. Come, soft god, come—
if I have planted ache into the scarred

earth of a man's skull, it's only that
I soothed him with the leather of my gloves.

The First Word

Her breath swung open like a broken shell:
and there, held in the blister of damp air
between her foreteeth and her tongue, it was—

no call; no song; no prayer; no jagged spell:
it was an emblem housed in sound, a palm
pressed from the ochre palette of her mouth

into the cave wall of his skull: it was
not *yes*, or *you*, or *hawk*, or *love*; just *look*,
and, when he did, the word dissolved.

As in the Love Songs of Moorish Spain

1.

You are a scent of water
        in the grass I reorder
walking barefoot
toward the boar's tusk of the moon.

2.

All night we lie along the hillside
watching constellations,
                    keeping stars up
        that would fall into the fields
but for each buttress
            arcing from our eyes.

3.

Copper, silver, bronze,
            so many bracelets
on your arms;
            like underwater coins,
            they scatter light
into the whirlpool

of the darkness
at the bottom of the sky.

After Love

She sleeps folded
up like an old phone
number, no name

on a scrap of nap-
kin in a stranger's calf-
skin wallet, her

half-closed hand
fleshy and pink
as a shaved lamb.

She is the seed
ingrown, alone
inside an avocado.

Her heart: a handful
of feathers
rubber-banded together:

a dandelion dismantled
by a breeze too cold to keep
to the East Coast.

Starfish quiver in her
head: slow rowboat
floating on the bed.

Collapse, Collapse

After Virgil, Aeneid *IV*

Citizen and tool fell   to disuse: a new rust
bloomed, saffron   as lichen on the hammer's edge,
dulling the hard spark   of noon, embellishing
the nail's head   and the saw's raw tooth

Passing sands dragged through   the outskirt alleys
troubling nothing   but the polish from a few
unfinished flights of stairs,   used now
only by stray pigeons   and the second-story air

Marble blocks once startled   from the quarries,
cut and carried to the capital   the queen misplaced,
took refuge from their purpose   Monday mornings
in the white sun of a city   love erased

Last Postcard from Pompeii

After Horace, Odes, *I.25*

The pebbles fell like grapes
or rain, pestering the windowpane
until you were awake.

The moon slid its small blue
hands into the bedroom, past you,
or it used to,

when the couplet of your shutters,
so often closed and opened, was
a butterfly, a flutter,

like the motions of your lovers,
frog's-legs kicking off the covers,
auguring motherhood.

You learned to make out
midnight's faces from its softly other shapes,
to separate

the thin-string song of crickets
from hoarse whispers
from your mates,

to guide an adolescent eyebrow
to your collarbone: a place
to sleep, a place.

Lady, quaking naked, waiting:
you were a station
taking in her train.

Grown old, now staling slowly,
loafing like a winter coat
thrown over a cold sofa,

you're alone. And you can't keep
a street cat. But the damp-handed rain
cramps the puddles,

smacks on ponchoed backs
and cackles
on a standing taxi.

Only dogs, walkers,
leaves and others' lovers
lift their sounds in through your shutters:

not whispers, but the lisping
winds, when leaves' husks scuttle
on the street: a sweep

of scarab beetles.

On Her Collarbone

Bone starlight yawns and then rejoices
in its trough, pale as a piano
key: the seam between her sleeping
and the bedroom's empty blackbox

theater, where nerve endings rehearse,
botching their lines—brashly off-book—
for the mind's prop comedy. I, too,
could shut my eyes, but then who would

describe the shadow of the shadow
of the night, gathered like black water
in the dent behind her clavicle,
the dreamer's only undulation

in the velvet stillness that reclines
above half-life? She gurgles, turning
over, and is blind; the bath spills
from its little tub. The bone itself

glows like a thread of cloud unwinding
through the winter sky. Her eyelids
flutter. She is quiet. The curtain
holds the starlight but the stars are held

outside. The stars seem motionless. She
sighs. Does time spread out through motion,
or does motion spread through time? I am
talking to myself. She murmurs

to her shoulder and then turns onto
her side: the bone rolls from the light.
The stars I count are burning out
into the fanning membrane of space-time.

Land's End

When did you wake? The sheets, still
softened by your sleep, are tousled

now, and almost cold; I turned
and, where your warmth was, all

was winter's pall when I returned.
Come back, and lay your shiver down

beside me in this open bed; there
is no safety in the world outside

this quilt, this pillow, this bare thread.
Lie here, and let me braid your hair

until my hands are veined and old
and weathered as the fisherman's,

whose fingers cast an ancient net
into a brightness they can't hold.

To One Waiting to Be Born

1.

Know your origin: you are a token
of the afterwards of love. What flinches
in the ribbon of your utterly new blood
is nothing but the echo of a bed post—
pulse.
       You have grown up. From filament
within your mother's bulb, you have evolved
into a chandelier of bones, weightlessly
orbiting your portion of the womb, aglow
in skin that holds you as an astronaut's
upholstery. Small ghost, your figure
is almost your own. You fidget, but
be still. Be whole. Rotate like a globe
until, too old, you can't be steadfasted
by axes. Your center has already lost
its poles.

2.

       Soon you will be divulged.
Good luck: you won't be born as much
as you'll be given up. And as you tumble
from your orbit toward this crib of sticks

and dust, be adamant. Be tough. All earth
is but a roughness underfoot. To be delivered
is too little and too much: it is the touch
that will disfigure you that you must learn
to touch. You will scuff and stain and ruin
like a patent leather boot, and stagger
haplessly through weather that gnarls
what is new. Your first face will be forgotten
as a field is under snow, and you will
let yourself be vandalized as all handsomeness
will. There is no balm for what is rotten,
and you will spoil like a plum, but still
wash every day and wash again the rancid
blemish that your body has become.

Stare into your hands.
How can you doubt that you are animal?

3.

Boy, this is your ontology: you are
because you must be someone's child.
Be otherwise. Be wild: be stranger
and more formless than a son.

          Cast off
the membrane that has covered you,
unwind the muscle that encumbers
you, and rise:
          twirl as a whirlwind
overhead, effortlessly aerial,
incorporeal, almost electrical—
drift as a bright curl in the bluish light
of sky: impervious, indifferent, unhuman.

Indirect Light

i.m. Michael Chapman (1978-1995)

The only earth we knew
then was the earth
            we would outgrow—
the screech owl's talon drawn
on parchment light,
            a yellow bulb
above the porch moths, an hour
there in the indistinct
            navy tablecloth
of night, running our hands
through it, rinsing our fingers
            as with lake water
in a winter without frost—
there in the weight of it,
            in the air between
pine needles and the rocks
sinking, even then, though
            imperceptibly,
into the tread of sucking mud,
we couldn't think of it,
            raised as we had been
once from the wet husks
of our mothers, lifted
            as by wind

and wound in bed sheets
warm as blood, we couldn't
                    think of it—
if we had known, we could have
huddled, held ourselves
                    and held each other,
we could have held each breath
until it clenched like granite
                    to the riverbed
of lung—but there, unknown
to us, it was, as tenderly
                    indefinite
as love, a death embedded
in the bright bead of each firefly
                    we cupped
out of the darkness with our palms
as soft as tongues, there
                    as our laughter
flapped above us like a swan—
it was, it was, it was, it was

Acknowledgments

Grateful acknowledgments are made to the editors of the following journals, in which a number of these poems first appeared, sometimes in alternate versions and under earlier titles:

32 Poems, The American Poetry Review, The Baffler, The Believer, Bennington Review, Ex/Post, Full Bleed, Gulf Coast, The Hopkins Review, Horsethief, Image, The Iowa Review, The Los Angeles Review of Books Quarterly Journal, Narrative, The Paris Review, Ploughshares, Poem-a-Day (The Academy of American Poets), Prairie Schooner, RealPoetik, The Southern Review, and Terminus.

"A Letter from the End of Days (Come In. Clean the House. We Have Died.)" also appeared on Poetry Daily and was set as a choral piece by composer Ching-chu Hu for the Ann Arbor Vocal Arts Ensemble, premiering May 2018.

"Prayer of the Last Prizefighter" was also featured on the Belfast [U.K.] Poetry Jukebox, installed March 2019, and appeared in Dutch translation by Menno van der Beek in Liter.

"For the Suburban Dead" was reprinted on Verse Daily.

"Indirect Light [Streetlights were our stars]" and "Indirect Light [The only earth we knew]" were included in *In the Tempered Dark: Contemporary Poets Transcending Elegy* (Black Lawrence Press, 2023).

The epigraph from Virgil's *Aeneid* (VI, 126-9) is translated by Seamus Heaney (lines 174-7 in the English rendering).

The epigraph by Simone Weil is from *Gravity and Grace*, translated by Emma Crawford.

Special thanks to all of the institutions and individuals instrumental to the making of this book, including the Amy Clampitt House, Birutė Ona Black, Jericho Brown, George David Clark, the Corporation of Yaddo, Brandon Courtney, Adam O. Davis, Four Way Books, Daniel Grossman, Ching-chu Hu, Andrew Hudgins, Kimberly Johnson, Ilya Kaminsky, Michael Lavers, Maurice Manning, Michael McGriff, Andrew Meredith, Matt W. Miller, Ryan Murphy, the National Endowment for the Arts, Jacqueline Osherow, Carmen Radley, Paisley Rekdal, the Sewanee Writers' Conference, Ed Skoog, Eric Smith, the University of San Diego, Matthew Yeager, and Dean Young. Abiding love both to my parents and to my wife Birutė, mano širdelė, mano meilė, without whom I would sound a lesser song.

About the Author

Malachi Black is also the author of *Storm Toward Morning* •
(Copper Canyon Press, 2014), a finalist for the Poetry Society of
America's Norma Farber First Book Award and a selection for
the PSA's New American Poets Series (chosen by Ilya Kaminsky).
Black's poems have appeared in *The American Poetry Review,*
The Believer, The Los Angeles Review of Books, The Paris Review,
Ploughshares, and *Poetry,* among other journals, and in a number
of anthologies, including *Before the Door of God: An Anthology*
of Devotional Poetry (Yale UP, 2013), *The Poet's Quest for God*
(Eyewear Publishing [U.K.], 2016), and *In the Tempered Dark:*
Contemporary Poets Transcending Elegy (Black Lawrence, 2023).
Black's work has been supported by fellowships and awards from
the Amy Clampitt House, the Bread Loaf Writers' Conference,
Emory University, the Fine Arts Work Center in Provincetown,
Hawthornden Castle, MacDowell, the National Endowment for
the Arts, the Poetry Foundation (a 2009 Ruth Lilly Fellowship),
the Sewanee Writers' Conference, and Yaddo. Black's poems
have several times been set to music and have been featured
in exhibitions both in the U.S. and abroad, including recent
and forthcoming translations into French, Dutch, Croatian,
Slovenian, and Lithuanian. Black teaches at the University of San
Diego and lives in California.

WE ARE ALSO GRATEFUL TO THOSE INDIVIDUALS WHO PARTICIPATED IN
OUR BUILD A BOOK PROGRAM. THEY ARE:

Anonymous (14), Robert Abrams, Debra Allbery, Nancy Allen,
Michael Ansara, Kathy Aponick, Jean Ball, Sally Ball, Jill Bialosky,
Sophie Cabot Black, Laurel Blossom, Tommye Blount, Karen and
David Blumenthal, Jonathan Blunk, Lee Briccetti, Jane Martha Brox,
Mary Lou Buschi, Anthony Cappo, Carla and Steven Carlson, Robin
Rosen Chang, Liza Charlesworth, Peter Coyote, Elinor Cramer, Kwame
Dawes, Michael Anna de Armas, Brian Komei Dempster, Renko and
Stuart Dempster, Matthew DeNichilo, Rosalynde Vas Dias, Patrick
Donnelly, Charles R. Douthat, Lynn Emanuel, Blas Falconer, Laura
Fjeld, Carolyn Forché, Helen Fremont and Donna Thagard, Debra
Gitterman, Dorothy Tapper Goldman, Alison Granucci, Elizabeth
T. Gray, Jr., Naomi Guttman and Jonathan Meade, Jeffrey Harrison,
KT Herr, Carlie Hoffman, Melissa Hotchkiss, Thomas and Autumn
Howard, Catherine Hoyser, Elizabeth Jackson, Linda Susan Jackson,
Jessica Jacobs, Deborah Jonas-Walsh, Jennifer Just, Voki Kalfayan,
Maeve Kinkead, Victoria Korth, David Lee and Jamila Trindle, Rodney
Terich Leonard, Howard Levy, Owen Lewis and Susan Ennis, Eve Linn,
Matthew Lippman, Ralph and Mary Ann Lowen, Maja Lukic, Neal
Lulofs, Anthony Lyons, Ricardo Alberto Maldonado, Trish Marshall,
Donna Masini, Deborah McAlister, Carol Moldaw, Michael and Nancy
Murphy, Kimberly Nunes, Matthew Olzmann and Vivee Francis,
Veronica Patterson, Patrick Phillips, Robert Pinsky, Megan Pinto,
Kevin Prufer, Anna Duke Reach, Paula Rhodes, Yoana Setzer, James
Shalek, Soraya Shalforoosh, Peggy Shinner, Joan Silber, Jane Simon,
Debra Spark, Donna Spruijt-Metz, Arlene Stang, Page Hill Starzinger,
Catherine Stearns, Yerra Sugarman, Arthur Sze, Laurence Tancredi,
Marjorie and Lew Tesser, Peter Turchi, Connie Voisine, Susan Walton,
Martha Webster and Robert Fuentes, Calvin Wei, Allison Benis White,
Lauren Yaffe, and Rolf Yngve.